GRANDMA'S
FAMILY MEALS

GRANDMA'S
FAMILY MEALS

DELICIOUS RECIPES FROM GRANDMA'S KITCHEN

This edition published in 2013
LOVE FOOD is an imprint of Parragon Books Ltd

Parragon
Chartist House
15–17 Trim Street
Bath, BA1 1HA, UK

Copyright © Parragon Books Ltd 2012

LOVE FOOD and the accompanying heart device is a trademark
of Parragon Books Ltd in Australia, the UK, USA, India, and the EU.

www.parragon.com/lovefood

All rights reserved. No part of this publication may be reproduced, stored in a retrleval system, or
transmitted, in any form or by any means, electronic, mechanical, photocopying, recording, or otherwise,
without the prior permission of the copyright holder.

ISBN: 978-1-78186-808-9

Printed in China

Introduction and Grandma's tips written by Linda Doeser
New recipes by Beverly LeBlanc
Edited by Fiona Biggs
Additional photography and styling by Mike Cooper
Additional home economy by Lincoln Jefferson
Internal design by Sarah Knight

Notes for the Reader
This book uses standard kitchen measuring spoons and cups. All spoon and cup measurements are
level unless otherwise indicated. Unless otherwise stated, milk is assumed to be whole, eggs are large,
individual vegetables are medium, and pepper is freshly ground black pepper. Unless otherwise stated, all
root vegetables should be washed and peeled before using.

Garnishes and serving suggestions are all optional and not necessarily included in the recipe ingredients
or method. The times given are only an approximate guide. Preparation times differ according to the
techniques used by different people and the cooking times may also vary from those given. Optional
ingredients, variations, or serving suggestions have not been included in the calculations.

Recipes using raw or very lightly cooked eggs should be avoided by infants, the elderly, pregnant women,
and people with weakened immune systems. Pregnant and breast-feeding women are advised to avoid
eating peanuts and peanut products. People with nut allergies should be aware that some of the prepared
ingredients used in the recipes in this book may contain nuts. Always check the packaging before use.
Vegetarians should be aware that some of the prepared ingredients used in the recipes in this book may
contain animal products. Always check the package before use.

Picture acknowledgments
The publisher would like to thank the following for permission to reproduce copyright material:
Vintage labels © AKaiser/Shutterstock
Close-up notepaper on cork board © Picsfive/Shutterstock
A coffee cup stain © Tyler Olson/Shutterstock
Masking tape © Samantha Grandy/Shutterstock
Vintage prints supplied courtesy of Istock Images

Contents

Introduction 6

Grandma's Comfort Food 8

Grandma's Winter Warmers 26

Grandma's Dinners To Delight 44

Grandma's Weekend Treats 62

Index 80

INTRODUCTION

Like just about every skill, cooking becomes easier, quicker, and better the more you do it. One of the great things about grandmas is that they have had a great amount of experience and have been doing the things they do—whether soothing a fractious baby or rustling up a meal for unexpected guests— for a long time. It would be foolish to not benefit from all the knowledge grandmas have gained over the years, with their immense repertoire of tips, tricks, and shortcuts for preparing delicious, attractive, appetizing, nutritional, and, often, budget-conscious meals for all the family.

This book is not just a superb collection of delicious recipes or even a nostalgic trip  through the warm memories of childhood, but a compilation of the collected culinary wisdom of many grandmas and grandmas' grandmas. Traditional recipes have been handed down the generations, tweaked and adjusted and then adapted to make full use of modern kitchens and equipment and to incorporate our contemporary range of ingredients without losing their uniquely special home-cooked qualities.

And there is nothing better than delicious home-cooked food, whether a hearty stew on a winter's evening, a comforting bowl of soup when you're feeling down, a quick-and-easy midweek meal, or a Sunday special with all the family. Grandmas know just how to prepare food that looks and smells wonderful, tastes superb, and satisfies the appetite. However, they no more want to spend hours in a steamy kitchen working over a hot stove than anyone else, so all these recipes are easy to follow and do not require any special skills—just good, old-fashioned common sense.

The recipes are divided into four chapters. Grandma's Comfort Food offers ideas for quick and easy lunches, simple dinners, and any-time-of-day snacks. For old-fashioned family favorites, turn to Grandma's Winter Warmers, with its mouthwatering collection of satisfying, hearty meals. Grandma's Dinners to Delight will certainly do just that, whether your preference is for pasta, meat, or fish—not to mention faultless crisp and golden fries. When you have a little more time, explore Grandma's Weekend Treats and rediscover the enjoyment of a Sunday roast, the simple but elegant pleasure of poached salmon, and how to cook their accompaniments to melt-in-the-mouth perfection.

Never have recipes been so tried and tested—the best of the old ways have been combined with the new, so you are virtually guaranteed success on a plate.

Chicken Noodle Soup

SERVES 4–6

INGREDIENTS

- 2 skinless, boneless chicken breasts
- 5 cups water or chicken stock
- 3 carrots, peeled and sliced into 1/4-inch slices
- 3 ounces egg noodles
- salt and pepper
- fresh tarragon leaves, to garnish

1 Place the chicken breasts in a large saucepan over medium heat, add the water, and bring to a simmer. Cook for 25–30 minutes. Skim any foam from the surface. Remove the chicken from the stock and check the chicken is tender and the juices run clear when the point of a sharp knife is inserted into the thickest part of the meat. Keep the chicken warm.

2 Continue to simmer the stock, add the carrots and noodles, and cook for 4–5 minutes.

3 Thinly slice or shred the chicken breasts and place in warm serving bowls.

4 Season the soup with salt and pepper and pour over the chicken. Serve immediately, garnished with the tarragon.

GRANDMA'S TIP
Clean hands are the fastest tools for shredding cooked chicken, flaking cooked fish, crumbling cheese, and tearing delicate salad greens and herbs.

Steak Sandwiches

SERVES 4

INGREDIENTS

- 8 slices thick white or whole-wheat bread
- butter, for spreading
- 2 handfuls mixed salad greens
- 3 tablespoons olive oil
- 2 onions, thinly sliced
- 1½ pounds top sirloin steak or tenderloin steak, about 1 inch thick
- 1 tablespoon Worcestershire sauce
- 2 tablespoons whole-grain mustard
- 2 tablespoons water
- salt and pepper

1 Spread each slice of bread with some butter and add some salad greens to half of the slices.

2 Heat 2 tablespoons of the oil in a large, heavy skillet over medium heat. Add the onions and cook, stirring occasionally, for 10–15 minutes, until softened and golden brown. Using a slotted spoon, transfer to a plate and set aside.

3 Increase the heat to high and add the remaining oil to the skillet. Add the steak, season with pepper and cook quickly on both sides to seal. Reduce the heat to medium and cook, turning once, for 2½–3 minutes each side for rare or 3½–5 minutes each side for medium. Transfer the steak to a plate.

4 Add the Worcestershire sauce, mustard, and water to the skillet and stir to deglaze by scraping any sediment from the bottom of the skillet. Return the onions to the skillet, season with salt and pepper, and mix well.

5 Thinly slice the steak across the grain, place on top of the salad greens, and cover with the onions. Cover with the remaining slice of bread and press down gently. Serve immediately.

FEEL-BETTER FOOD

Scalloped Potatoes

SERVES 8

INGREDIENTS

- 1 tablespoon salted butter, plus extra for greasing
- 1 tablespoon all-purpose flour
- 1 cup heavy cream
- 2 cups whole milk
- 1 teaspoon salt
- pinch of freshly grated nutmeg
- pinch of freshly ground white pepper
- 4 fresh thyme sprigs
- 2 garlic cloves, finely chopped
- 4½ pounds russet potatoes, thinly sliced
- 1 cup shredded white or orange cheddar cheese
- salt and pepper

1 Preheat the oven to 375°F. Grease a 15 × 10-inch ovenproof dish.

2 Melt the butter in a saucepan over medium heat. Stir in the flour and cook, stirring continuously, for 2 minutes. Gradually beat in the cream and milk and bring to simmering point. Add the salt, nutmeg, white pepper, thyme, and garlic, reduce the heat to low, and simmer for 5 minutes. Remove the thyme sprigs.

3 Make a layer with half of the potatoes in the prepared dish and season generously with salt and pepper. Top with half of the sauce and cover with half of the cheese. Repeat the layers with the remaining potatoes, sauce, and cheese.

4 Bake in the preheated oven for about 1 hour, or until the top is browned and the potatoes are tender. Remove from the oven and let rest for 15 minutes before serving.

GRANDMA'S TIP
These creamy, garlicky potatoes make the perfect side dish for any Sunday roast.

Pizza Margherita

SERVES 6

INGREDIENTS

PIZZA DOUGH
- 4½ teaspoons active dry yeast
- 1 teaspoon sugar
- 1 cup lukewarm water
- 2½ cups white bread flour, plus extra for dusting
- 1 teaspoon salt
- 1 tablespoon olive oil, plus extra for oiling

TOPPING
- 1 (14½-ounce) can diced tomatoes
- 2 garlic cloves, crushed
- 2 teaspoons dried basil
- 1 tablespoon olive oil
- 2 tablespoons tomato paste
- 1 cup chopped mozzarella cheese
- 2 tablespoons freshly grated Parmesan cheese
- salt and pepper
- fresh basil leaves, to garnish

PRACTICE MAKES PERFECT

1 Place the yeast and sugar in a small bowl and mix with ¼ cup of the water. Let the yeast mixture stand in a warm place for 15 minutes, or until frothy.

2 Mix the flour with the salt and make a well in the center. Add the oil, the yeast mixture, and the remaining water. Using a wooden spoon, mix to form a smooth dough.

3 Invert the dough onto a floured work surface and knead for 4–5 minutes, or until smooth.

4 Return the dough to the bowl, cover with a sheet of oiled plastic wrap, and let

rise for 30 minutes, or until doubled in size.

5 Knead the dough for 2 minutes. Stretch the dough with your hands, then place it on an oiled baking sheet or pizza stone, pushing out the edges until even. The dough should be no more than ¼ inch thick because it will rise during cooking.

6 Preheat the oven to 400°F. To make the topping, place the tomatoes, garlic, basil, and oil in a large skillet over medium heat, season with salt and pepper, and let simmer for 20 minutes, or until the sauce has thickened. Stir in the tomato paste and let cool slightly.

7 Spread the topping evenly over the pizza crust. Top with the mozzarella cheese and Parmesan cheese and bake in the preheated oven for 20–25 minutes. Serve immediately, garnished with basil leaves.

Creamy Salmon Baked Potatoes

SERVES 4

INGREDIENTS

- 4 russet potatoes (about 10 ounces each), scrubbed
- 8 ounces skinless salmon fillet
- 1 cup cream cheese
- 2–3 tablespoons skim milk
- 2 tablespoons chopped/snipped fresh herbs, such as dill or chives
- ½ cup shredded cheddar cheese or American cheese
- salt and pepper

1 Preheat the oven to 400°F. Prick the skins of the potatoes and place on the top shelf of the preheated oven. Bake for 50–60 minutes, until the skins are crisp and the centers are soft when pierced with a sharp knife.

2 Meanwhile, bring a saucepan of water to a boil, then reduce the heat until the water is simmering gently. Add the salmon fillet to the pan and cook for 4–5 minutes (if in one piece), or until just cooked but still moist. Alternatively, cut into 2–3 even pieces and cook in a microwave oven on Medium for 2 minutes, then turn the pieces around so that the cooked parts are in the center of the oven, and cook for an additional 1 minute, or until just cooked but still moist. Using a fork, flake the flesh into a bowl.

3 In a separate bowl, blend the cream cheese with just enough of the milk to loosen, then stir in the herbs and a little salt and pepper.

4 When the potatoes are cooked, preheat the broiler to high. Cut the potatoes in half lengthwise. Carefully scoop the potato flesh out of the skins, reserving the skins. Add the flesh to the cream cheese mixture and mash together. Lightly stir in the salmon flakes.

5 Spoon the filling into the potato skins and top with the cheese. Cook under the preheated broiler for 1–2 minutes, until the cheese is bubbling and turning golden. Serve immediately.

GRANDMA'S TIP
Make sure the potatoes are baked through so that they're soft inside and the skins are firm and crispy, which makes them delicious. You can rub salt into the skins with oil to enhance the flavor.

Macaroni & Cheese

SERVES 4

INGREDIENTS

- 8 ounces dried macaroni pasta
- 2½ cups whole milk
- ½ teaspoon grated nutmeg
- 4 tablespoons salted butter, plus extra for cooking the pasta
- ½ cup all-purpose flour
- 1¾ cups shredded sharp cheddar cheese
- ½ cup grated Parmesan cheese
- 1 (6-ounce) package baby spinach
- salt and pepper

1 Cook the macaroni according to the package directions. Remove from the heat, drain, stir in a small pat of butter to keep it soft, return to the saucepan, and cover to keep warm.

2 Put the milk and nutmeg into a saucepan over low heat and heat until warm, but don't boil. Put the butter into a heavy saucepan over low heat, melt the butter, add the flour, and stir to make a paste. Cook gently for 2 minutes. Add the warm milk a little at a time, beating it into the paste, then cook for about 10–15 minutes to make a sauce.

3 Add three-quarters of the cheddar cheese and Parmesan cheese and stir through until they have melted in, then add the spinach, season with salt and pepper, and remove from the heat.

4 Preheat the broiler to high. Put the macaroni into a shallow heatproof dish, then pour the sauce over the pasta. Sprinkle the remaining cheese over the top and place the dish under the preheated broiler. Broil until the cheese begins to brown, then serve immediately.

GRANDMA'S TIP
You can add texture to this by sprinkling some whole-wheat bread crumbs over the cheese before placing under the broiler.

Homemade Hamburgers

SERVES 6

INGREDIENTS

- 2¼ pounds fresh ground beef
- I small onion, grated
- I tablespoon chopped fresh parsley
- 2 teaspoons Worcestershire sauce
- 2 tablespoons sunflower oil
- salt and pepper

TO SERVE

- 6 burger buns, halved and toasted
- lettuce leaves
- tomato slices
- pickle slices
- ketchup

1 Put the beef, onion, and parsley into a bowl, add the Worcestershire sauce, season with salt and pepper, and mix well with your hands until thoroughly combined.

2 Divide the mixture into six equal portions and shape into balls, then gently flatten into patties. If you have time, chill in the refrigerator for 30 minutes until firm. Meanwhile, preheat the oven to low.

3 Heat the oil in a large skillet. Add the patties, in batches, and cook over medium heat for 5–8 minutes on each side, turning them carefully with a spatula. Remove from the skillet and keep warm in the preheated oven while you cook the remaining burgers.

4 Serve in toasted buns with lettuce, tomato slices, pickles, and ketchup.

GRANDMA'S GUILTY PLEASURE

GRANDMA'S TIP
Make a large batch and freeze, individually wrapped or stored in a plastic container with parchment paper between the burgers to keep them separate.

Barbecue-Glazed Drumsticks

SERVES 6

INGREDIENTS

- 12 chicken drumsticks (about 3½ pounds)
- 1 cup barbecue sauce
- 1 tablespoon packed light brown sugar
- 1 tablespoon cider vinegar
- 1 teaspoon salt
- ½ teaspoon pepper
- ½ teaspoon Tabasco sauce
- vegetable oil, for brushing

1 Using a sharp knife, make 2 slashes, about 1 inch apart, into the thickest part of the drumsticks, cutting to the bone. Put the drumsticks into a large, sealable plastic freezer bag.

2 Mix together ¼ cup of the barbecue sauce, the sugar, vinegar, salt, pepper, and Tabasco sauce in a small bowl. Pour the mixture into the bag, press out most of the air, and seal tightly. Shake the bag gently to distribute the sauce evenly and let marinate in the refrigerator for at least 4 hours.

3 Preheat the oven to 400°F. Line a baking sheet with alumnium foil and brush lightly with oil.

4 Using tongs, transfer the drumsticks to the prepared baking sheet, spacing them evenly apart. Discard the marinade. Brush both sides of the drumsticks with some of the remaining barbecue sauce.

5 Bake for 15 minutes, then remove from the oven and brush generously with more barbecue sauce. Return to the oven and repeat this process three more times for a total cooking time of 1 hour. Cook until the chicken is tender and the juices run clear when the point of a sharp knife is inserted into the thickest part of the meat.

CHILDREN'S FAVORITE

GRANDMA'S WINTER WARMERS

Chicken Pot Pie

SERVES 6

INGREDIENTS

- 1 tablespoon olive oil
- 3 cups sliced white button mushrooms
- 1 onion, finely chopped
- 6 carrots, sliced
- 3 celery stalks, sliced
- 4 cups chicken stock
- 6 tablespoons salted butter
- ½ cup all-purpose flour, plus extra for dusting
- 2 pounds skinless, boneless chicken breasts, cut into 1-inch cubes
- ⅔ cup frozen peas
- 1 teaspoon chopped fresh thyme or a pinch of dried thyme
- 3 (9-inch) store-bought rolled dough pie crusts, thawed, if frozen
- 1 egg, lightly beaten
- salt and pepper

1 Heat the olive oil in a large saucepan over medium heat. Add the mushrooms and onion and cook, stirring frequently, for about 8 minutes, until golden. Add the carrots, celery, and half of the stock and bring to a boil. Reduce the heat to low and simmer for 12–15 minutes, until the vegetables are almost tender.

2 Melt the butter in another large saucepan over medium heat. Whisk in the flour and cook, stirring continuously, for 4 minutes, until the flour is light tan in color. Gradually beat in the remaining chicken stock. Reduce the heat to medium–low and simmer, stirring, until thickened.

3 Stir in the vegetable mixture, add the chicken, peas, and thyme, and season with salt and pepper. Bring back to a simmer and cook, stirring continuously, for 5 minutes. Taste and adjust the seasoning, if necessary, and remove from the heat. Preheat the oven to 400°F.

4 Divide the filling among six large ramekins (individual ceramic dishes), filling them to within ½ inch of the top. Roll out the dough on a lightly floured work surface and cut out six circles 1 inch larger than the diameter of the ramekins.

5 Put the circles on top of the filling, then fold over ½ inch all the way around to make a rim. Pinch with your fingertips to form a crimped edge, if desired. Cut a small cross in the center of each crust.

6 Put the ramekins on a baking sheet and brush the tops with the beaten egg. Bake in the preheated oven for 35–40 minutes, until the pies are golden brown and bubbling. Remove from the oven and let cool for 15 minutes before serving.

GRANDMA'S TIP
To thaw phyllo pastry quickly, separate the sheets and cover each one in plastic wrap; let the sheets thaw at room temperature for 30 minutes.

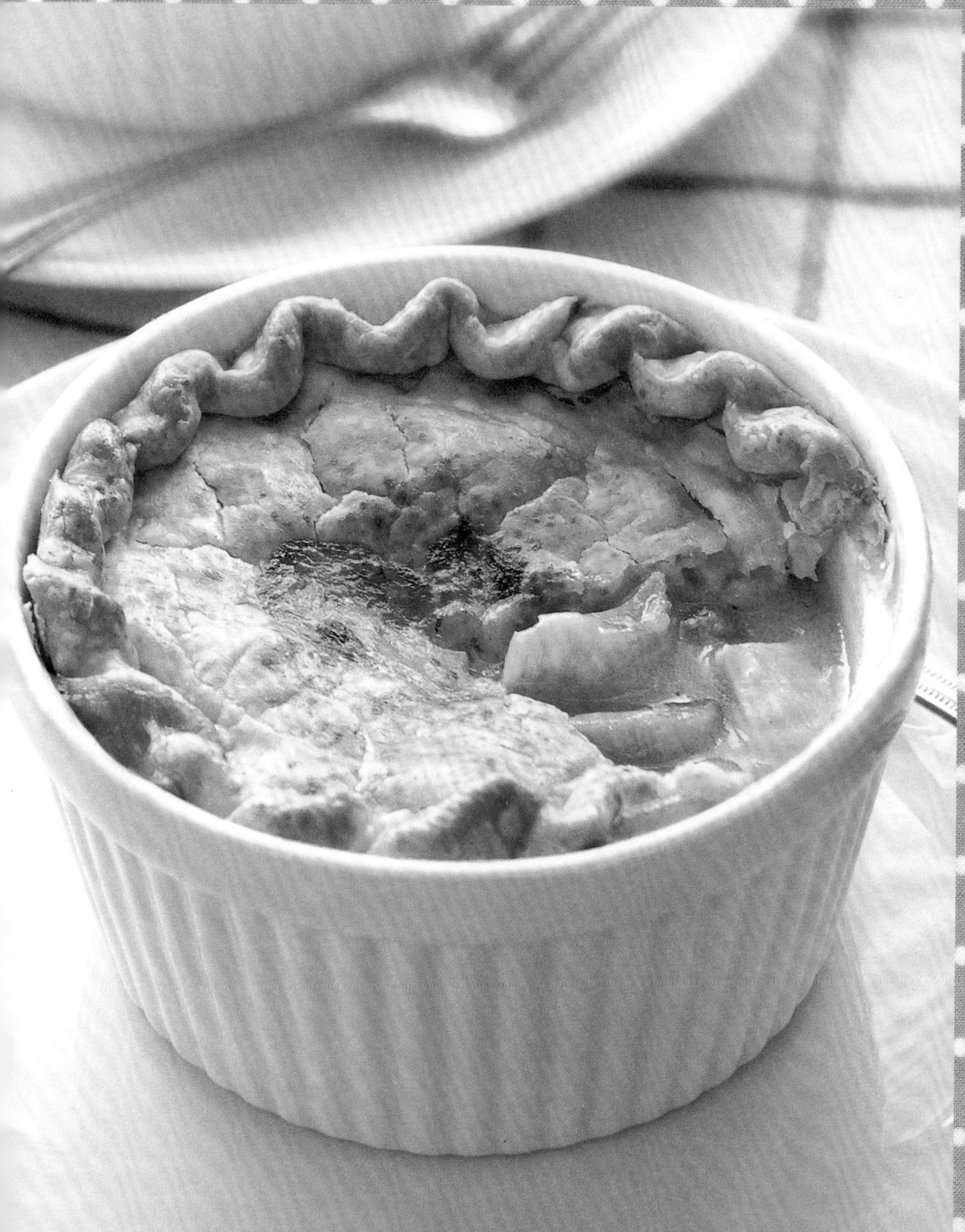

Tuna & Pasta Casserole

SERVES 4–6

INGREDIENTS

- 8 ounces dried ribbon egg pasta, such as tagliatelle
- 2 tablespoons salted butter
- 1¼ cups fine fresh bread crumbs
- 1 (14½-ounce) can condensed cream of mushroom soup
- ½ cup whole milk
- 2 celery stalks, chopped
- 1 red bell pepper, seeded and chopped
- 1 green bell pepper, seeded and chopped
- 1¼ cups shredded sharp cheddar cheese
- 2 tablespoons chopped fresh parsley
- 1 (5-ounce) can chunk light tuna in oil, drained and flaked
- salt and pepper

1 Preheat the oven to 400°F. Bring a large saucepan of lightly salted water to a boil. Add the pasta, bring back to a boil, and cook for 2 minutes less than specified on the package directions.

2 Meanwhile, melt the butter in a separate small saucepan. Stir in the bread crumbs, then remove from the heat and set aside.

3 Drain the pasta well and set aside. Pour the soup into the pasta pan, set over medium heat, then stir in the milk, celery, red bell pepper, green bell pepper, half of the cheese, and all the parsley.

4 Add the tuna and gently stir in so that the flakes don't break up. Season with salt and pepper. Heat just until small bubbles appear around the edge of the mixture—do not boil.

5 Stir the pasta into the pan and use two forks to mix all the ingredients together. Spoon the mixture into an ovenproof dish that is also suitable for serving and spread it out.

6 Stir the remaining cheese into the buttered bread crumbs, then sprinkle it over the top of the pasta mixture. Bake in the preheated oven for 20–25 minutes, until the topping is golden. Remove from the oven, then let stand for 5 minutes before serving straight from the dish.

DELICIOUS & ECONOMICAL

Hearty Beef Stew

SERVES 4

INGREDIENTS

- 3 pounds boneless chuck steak, cut into 2-inch pieces
- 2 tablespoons vegetable oil
- 2 onions, cut into 1-inch pieces
- 3 tablespoons all-purpose flour
- 3 garlic cloves, finely chopped
- 4 cups beef stock
- 3 carrots, cut into 1-inch lengths
- 2 celery stalks, cut into 1-inch lengths
- 1 tablespoon ketchup
- 1 bay leaf
- ¼ teaspoon dried thyme
- ¼ teaspoon dried rosemary
- 8 Yukon gold or white round potatoes (about 2 pounds), cut into large chunks
- salt and pepper

1 Season the steak very generously with salt and pepper. Heat the oil in a large flameproof casserole dish over high heat. When the oil begins to smoke slightly, add the steak, in batches, if necessary, and cook, stirring frequently, for 5–8 minutes, until well browned. Using a slotted spoon, transfer to a bowl.

2 Reduce the heat to medium, add the onions to the casserole dish, and cook, stirring occasionally, for 5 minutes, until translucent. Stir in the flour and cook, stirring continuously, for 2 minutes. Add the garlic and cook for 1 minute. Beat in

1 cup of the stock and cook, scraping up all the sediment from the bottom of the casserole dish, then stir in the remaining stock and add the carrots, celery, ketchup, bay leaf, thyme, rosemary, and 1 teaspoon of salt. Return the steak to the casserole dish.

3 Bring back to a gentle simmer, cover, and cook over low heat for 1 hour. Add the potatoes, cover the casserole dish again, and simmer for an additional 30 minutes. Remove the lid, increase the heat to medium, and cook, stirring occasionally, for an additional 30 minutes, or until the meat and vegetables are tender. Remove the bay leaf.

4 If the stew becomes too thick, add a little more stock or water and adjust the seasoning, if necessary. Let stand for 15 minutes before serving.

GRANDMA'S TIP
Chuck steak is a term used for several cuts of beef that are suited to long, slow cooking. Look for a marbling of fat through the meat, which will break down during cooking and add flavor.

Meatloaf

SERVES 6–8
INGREDIENTS

- 2 carrots, diced
- 1 celery stalk, diced
- 1 onion, diced
- 1 red bell pepper, seeded and chopped
- 4 large white mushrooms, sliced
- 2 tablespoons salted butter
- 1 tablespoon olive oil, plus extra for brushing
- 3 garlic cloves, peeled and chopped
- 1 teaspoon dried thyme
- 2 teaspoons finely chopped rosemary
- 1 teaspoon Worcestershire sauce
- ¼ cup ketchup
- ½ teaspoon cayenne pepper
- 2½ pounds ground beef, chilled
- 2 teaspoons salt
- 1 teaspoon pepper
- 2 eggs, beaten
- 1¼ cups fresh bread crumbs
- green peas and Mashed Potatoes (see page 74), to serve

GLAZE

- 2 tablespoons packed brown sugar
- 2 tablespoons ketchup
- 1 tablespoon Dijon mustard

1. Put the vegetables into a food processor and pulse until finely chopped, scraping down the bowl several times with a spatula.

2. Melt the butter with the oil and garlic in a large skillet. Add the vegetable mixture and cook over medium heat, stirring frequently, for about 10 minutes, until most of the moisture has evaporated and the mixture is lightly caramelized.

3. Remove the skillet from the heat and stir in the thyme, rosemary, Worcestershire sauce, ketchup, and cayenne pepper. Let cool to room temperature.

4. Preheat the oven to 325°F. Lightly brush a shallow roasting pan with olive oil.

5. Put the beef into a large bowl and gently break it up with your fingertips. Add the cooled vegetable mixture, salt, pepper, and eggs, and mix gently with your fingers for just 30 seconds. Add the bread crumbs and continue to mix until combined. The less you work the meat, the better the texture of the meatloaf.

6. Put the meatloaf mixture in the center of the prepared roasting pan, dampen your hands with cold water, and shape it into a loaf about 6 inches wide by 4 inches high. Dampen your hands again and smooth the surface. Bake in the center of the preheated oven for 30 minutes.

7. Meanwhile, make the glaze. Beat together the brown sugar, ketchup, Dijon mustard, and a pinch of salt in a small bowl.

8. Remove the meatloaf from the oven and spread the glaze evenly over the top with a spoon and spread some down the sides as well. Return to the oven and bake for an additional 35–45 minutes, or until the internal temperature reaches 155°F on a meat thermometer. Remove and let rest for at least 15 minutes before slicing thickly to serve. Serve with peas and Mashed Potatoes.

HEART WARMING FOOD

Sausages & Mashed Potatoes

SERVES 4

INGREDIENTS

- I tablespoon olive oil
- 8 good-quality link sausages
- Mashed Potatoes (see page 74), to serve

ONION GRAVY
- 3 onions, halved and thinly sliced
- 5 tablespoons salted butter
- ¼ cup Marsala or port
- ½ cup vegetable stock
- salt and pepper

1 Place the oil in a skillet over low heat and add the sausages. Cover the skillet and cook for 25–30 minutes, turning the sausages from time to time, until browned all over.

2 Meanwhile, prepare the onion gravy by placing the onions in a skillet with the butter and sautéing over low heat until soft, stirring continuously. Continue to cook for about 30 minutes, or until the onions are brown and have started to caramelize.

3 Pour in the Marsala and stock and continue to bubble away until the onion gravy is really thick. Season with salt and pepper.

4 Serve the sausages immediately with the Mashed Potatoes, with the onion gravy spooned over them.

GRANDMA'S TIP
When cooking a lot of sausages, thread them onto skewers before putting them under the broiler or on the barbecue to make them easy to turn.

Chicken-Fried Steak

SERVES 4
INGREDIENTS

- 4 minute steaks, about
  6 ounces each
- 2 eggs, beaten
- 1/4 cup milk
- 1 cup all-purpose flour
- 1 tablespoon paprika
- 1/2 teaspoon white pepper
- vegetable oil, for frying
- salt and pepper
- Mashed Potatoes
  (see page 74), to serve

GRAVY
- 4 ounces bulk sausage or
  sausage meat removed
  from the casings
- 3 scallions, white parts
  chopped, green parts sliced
  and reserved to garnish
- 3 tablespoons butter
- 1/4 cup all-purpose flour
- 2 1/2 cups milk, plus extra
  if needed
- cayenne pepper

1 Generously season both sides of the steaks with salt and pepper. Put the eggs and milk into a shallow dish, beat together, and set aside. Put the flour, paprika, and white pepper into a second shallow dish and mix well to combine.

2 One at a time, dip the steaks into the egg mixture, turning to coat completely, and then dredge in the flour, coating on both sides. Place the egged and floured steaks on a plate and let stand for 10 minutes. Meanwhile, preheat the oven to low.

3 Add about 1/4 inch of oil to a large skillet and place over medium–high heat. When the oil begins to shimmer, add the steaks and cook for about 3–4 minutes on each side, until golden brown and cooked through.

4 Remove from the skillet and drain for about 2 minutes on a wire rack set over paper towels. If working in batches, keep the cooked steaks warm in the preheated oven until the remainder have been cooked.

5 To make the gravy, put the sausage meat into a medium saucepan, place over medium heat, and cook until browned, breaking up the meat into small pieces with a wooden spoon. Add the white parts of the scallion and the butter and sauté for a few minutes, until the onions are translucent.

6 Stir in the flour and cook for 3 minutes. Gradually beat in the milk until combined. When it reaches simmering point, reduce the heat to low and cook, stirring occasionally, for 15 minutes. If the gravy thickens too much, add some more milk. Season with cayenne pepper, salt, and pepper, and serve with the Mashed Potatoes, garnished with the green parts of the scallions.

Pork Chops with Applesauce

SERVES 4
INGREDIENTS

- 4 pork rib chops on the bone, about 1¼ inches thick, at room temperature
- 1½ tablespoons sunflower oil or canola oil
- salt and pepper

APPLESAUCE

- 3 cooking apples, such as Granny Smith, peeled, cored, and diced
- ¼ cup granulated sugar, plus extra, if needed
- finely grated zest of ½ lemon
- ½ tablespoon lemon juice, plus extra, if needed
- ¼ cup water
- ¼ teaspoon ground cinnamon
- pat of butter

1 Preheat the oven to 400°F.

2 To make the applesauce, put the apples, sugar, lemon zest, lemon juice, and water into a heavy saucepan over high heat and bring to a boil, stirring to dissolve the sugar. Reduce the heat to low, cover, and simmer for 15–20 minutes, until the apples are tender and fall apart when you mash them against the side of the pan. Stir in the cinnamon and butter and beat the apples until they are as smooth or chunky as you like. Stir in extra sugar or lemon juice, to taste. Remove the pan from the heat, cover, and keep the applesauce warm.

3 Meanwhile, pat the chops dry and season with salt and pepper. Heat the oil in a large ovenproof skillet over medium–high heat. Add the chops and cook for 3 minutes on each side to brown.

4 Transfer the skillet to the oven and roast the chops for 7–9 minutes, until cooked through and the juices run clear when you cut the chops. Remove the pan from the oven, cover with aluminum foil, and let stand for 3 minutes. Gently reheat the applesauce, if necessary.

5 Transfer the chops to warm plates and spoon the pan juices over them. Serve immediately, accompanied by the applesauce.

IMPRESS THE FAMILY

Old-Fashioned Chicken Stew

SERVES 6

INGREDIENTS

- 2 tablespoons vegetable oil
- 4–5-pound chicken, cut into quarters, backbone reserved
- 3 cups chicken stock
- 3 cups water
- 4 garlic cloves, peeled and chopped
- 1 bay leaf
- 4 fresh thyme sprigs
- 5 tablespoons salted butter
- 2 carrots, cut into ½-inch lengths
- 2 celery stalks, cut into ½-inch lengths
- 1 large onion, chopped
- ⅔ cup all-purpose flour
- 1½ teaspoons salt
- pepper
- dash of Tabasco sauce

DUMPLINGS

- 1⅔ cups all-purpose flour
- 1 teaspoon salt
- 2 teaspoons baking powder
- ¼ teaspoon baking soda
- 3 tablespoons salted butter, chilled
- 2 tablespoons thinly sliced scallions
- ¼ cup buttermilk
- ¾ cup whole milk

1 Put the oil into a large, heavy flameproof casserole dish, add the chicken pieces, and cook over high heat, turning frequently, for 10 minutes, until browned all over. Pour in the stock and water, add the garlic, bay leaf, and thyme, and bring to a boil.

2 Reduce the heat, cover, and simmer for 30 minutes. Remove the casserole dish from the heat, remove and discard the bay leaf, and transfer the chicken to a bowl and let cool. Strain the cooking liquid into another bowl and skim off any fat that rises to the surface.

3 Put the butter, carrots, celery, and onion into the casserole dish and cook over medium heat, stirring frequently, for 5 minutes. Stir in the flour and cook, stirring continuously, for 2 minutes. Gradually beat in the reserved cooking liquid, a ladleful at a time. Add the salt and some pepper and stir in the Tabasco sauce. Reduce the heat to low, cover, and simmer for 30 minutes, until the vegetables are tender.

4 Skin the chicken pieces and remove the meat from the bones, tearing it into bite-size chunks. Stir the chunks into the cooked vegetables, cover the casserole dish, and reduce the heat to the lowest possible setting.

5 To make the dumplings, sift together the flour, salt, baking powder, and baking soda into a bowl. Add the butter and cut in with a pastry blender or rub in with your fingertips until the mixture resembles coarse bread crumbs. Add the scallions, buttermilk, and milk and stir with a fork into a thick dough.

6 Increase the heat under the casserole dish to medium and stir well. Shape the dumpling dough into large balls and add to the casserole dish. Cover and simmer for 15 minutes, until the dumplings are firm and cooked in the middle. Remove from the heat and serve immediately.

GRANDMA'S DINNERS TO DELIGHT

Spaghetti alla Carbonara

SERVES 4

INGREDIENTS

- 1 pound dried spaghetti
- 1 tablespoon olive oil
- 8 ounces pancetta or bacon, chopped
- 4 eggs
- ⅓ cup light cream
- 2 tablespoons freshly grated Parmesan cheese
- salt and pepper

1 Bring a large saucepan of lightly salted water to a boil, add the pasta, bring back to a boil, and cook according to the package directions, until tender but still firm to the bite.

2 Meanwhile, heat the oil in a heavy skillet. Add the pancetta and cook over medium heat, stirring frequently, for 8–10 minutes.

3 Beat the eggs with the cream in a small bowl and season with salt and pepper. Drain the pasta and return it to the saucepan.

4 Add the contents of the skillet, then add the egg mixture and half of the cheese. Stir well, then transfer the spaghetti to a warm serving dish. Serve immediately, sprinkled with the remaining cheese.

GRANDMA'S TIP
Sprinkling salt over spilled red wine prevents the stain from spreading, but do not do this on a carpet, because you'll never remove the residue. Blot with paper towels instead.

Corned Beef Hash

SERVES 6

INGREDIENTS

- 2 tablespoons
  salted butter
- 1 tablespoon vegetable oil
- 1½ pounds corned beef,
  cut into small cubes
- 1 onion, diced
- 3 red-skinned or white
  round potatoes, cut into
  small cubes
- ¼ teaspoon paprika
- ¼ teaspoon garlic powder
- ¼ cup diced green bell
  pepper or jalapeño chiles
- 1 tablespoon snipped
  chives, plus extra to
  garnish
- salt and pepper
- 6 poached eggs, to serve

1 Put the butter, oil, corned beef, and onion into a large, cold, nonstick or heavy skillet. Place the skillet over medium–low heat and cook, stirring occasionally, for 10 minutes.

2 Meanwhile, bring a large saucepan of lightly salted water to a boil, add the potatoes, bring back to a boil, and cook for 5–7 minutes, until partly cooked but still firm. Drain well and add to the skillet, together with the remaining ingredients, excluding the eggs.

3 Mix together well and press down lightly with a spatula to flatten. Increase the heat to medium. Every 10 minutes, turn the mixture with a spatula to bring the crusty bottom up to the top. Do this several times until the mixture is well-browned, the potatoes have crisp edges, and the cubes of meat are caramelized.

4 Taste and adjust the seasoning, if necessary. Transfer to warm serving plates and top each with a poached egg. Garnish with chives and serve immediately.

DELICIOUS
&
ECONOMICAL

GRANDMA'S TIP
Quick to make and delicious to eat, this is perfect served with broiled tomatoes, peas, or baked beans. If you don't like corned beef, try using leftover cooked turkey or canned tuna.

Fish, French Fries & Peas

SERVES 4

INGREDIENTS

- vegetable oil, for deep-frying
- 6 large russet potatoes, peeled and cut into sticks
- 4 thick cod fillets, about 6 oz each

BATTER

- 1¾ cups all-purpose flour, plus extra for dusting
- 1¾ teaspoons baking powder
- ½ teaspoon salt
- 1¼ cups cold lager

MASHED PEAS

- 2½ cups frozen peas
- 2 tablespoons salted butter
- 2 tablespoons light cream
- salt and pepper

1 To make the batter, sift the flour and baking powder into a bowl with the salt and beat in most of the lager. Check the consistency and add the remaining lager; it should be thick, like heavy cream. Chill in the refrigerator for half an hour.

2 To make the mashed peas, bring a large saucepan of lightly salted water to a boil, add the peas, bring back to a boil, and cook for 3 minutes. Drain and mash to a thick puree, then add the butter and cream and season with salt and pepper. Set aside and keep warm while cooking the fish.

3 Heat the oil to 250°F in a thermostatically controlled deep-fat fryer or in a large saucepan using a thermometer. Preheat the oven to 300°F.

4 Add the potato sticks to the oil and cook for about 8–10 minutes, until softened but not colored. Remove from the oil, drain on paper towels, and place in a dish in the preheated oven. Increase the temperature of the oil to 350°F.

5 Season the fish with salt and pepper and dust lightly with a little flour. Dip one fillet in the batter and coat thickly.

6 Carefully place the fillet in the hot oil and repeat with the other fillets (you may need to do this in batches). Cook for 8–10 minutes, turning halfway through. Remove the fish from the oil, drain, and keep warm.

7 Reheat the oil to 350°F and recook the French fries for 2–3 minutes, until golden brown. Drain and season with salt and pepper. Serve immediately with the mashed peas.

> **GRANDMA'S TIP**
> Avoid overcrowding food in a deep-fat fryer or saucepan, because it will make the temperature of the oil drop. This increases the oil absorption, resulting in a soggy batter.

Pasta with Pesto

SERVES 4
INGREDIENTS

- 1 pound dried tagliatelle
- fresh basil leaves, to garnish

PESTO

- 2 garlic cloves
- 3 tablespoons pine nuts
- 5 cups fresh basil leaves
  (about 4 ounces)
- 2/3 cup freshly grated
  Parmesan cheese
- 1/2 cup olive oil
- salt

1 To make the pesto, put the garlic, pine nuts, a large pinch of salt, and the basil into a mortar and pound to a paste with a pestle. Transfer to a bowl and gradually work in the cheese with a wooden spoon, then add the olive oil to make a thick, creamy sauce. Taste and adjust the seasoning, if necessary.

2 Alternatively, put the garlic, pine nuts, and a large pinch of salt into a blender or food processor and process briefly. Add the basil and process to a paste. With the motor still running, gradually add the olive oil. Scrape into a bowl and beat in the cheese. Season with salt.

3 Bring a large saucepan of lightly salted water to a boil. Add the pasta, bring back to a boil and cook according to the package directions, or until tender but still firm to the bite.

4 Drain well, return to the saucepan, and toss with half of the pesto, then divide among warm serving plates and top with the remaining pesto. Garnish with the basil leaves and serve.

GRANDMA'S TIP
Try replacing the traditional tomato sauce on your homemade pizza with pesto, top with mozzarella, and bake.

Lasagna with Cheese Sauce

SERVES 6

INGREDIENTS

- 2 tablespoons olive oil
- 2 ounces pancetta or bacon, chopped
- 1 onion, chopped
- 1 garlic clove, chopped
- 8 ounces fresh ground beef
- 2 celery stalks, chopped
- 2 carrots, chopped
- pinch of sugar
- ½ teaspoon dried oregano
- 1 (14½-ounce) can diced tomatoes
- 8 ounces oven-ready lasagna noodles
- 1⅓ cups freshly grated Parmesan cheese, plus extra for sprinkling
- salt and pepper

CHEESE SAUCE

- 1¼ cups whole milk
- 1 bay leaf
- 6 black peppercorns
- slice of onion
- blade of mace
- 2 tablespoons butter
- 3 tablespoons all-purpose flour
- 2 teaspoons Dijon mustard
- 1½ cups shredded cheddar cheese

1 Preheat the oven to 375°F. Heat the oil in a large, heavy saucepan. Add the pancetta and cook over medium heat, stirring occasionally, for 3 minutes, or until the fat begins to run. Add the onion and garlic and cook, stirring occasionally, for 5 minutes, or until softened.

2 Add the beef and cook, breaking it up with a wooden spoon, until browned all over. Stir in the celery and carrots and cook for 5 minutes. Season with salt and pepper. Add the sugar, oregano, and tomatoes. Bring to a boil, reduce the heat to low, and simmer for 30 minutes.

3 Meanwhile, make the cheese sauce. Pour the milk into a saucepan and add the bay leaf, peppercorns, onion, and mace. Heat gently to just below boiling point, then remove from the heat, cover, and let steep for 10 minutes.

4 Strain the milk into a small bowl. Melt the butter in a clean saucepan. Sprinkle in the flour and cook over low heat, stirring continuously, for 1 minute. Remove from the heat and gradually stir in the warm milk. Return to the heat and bring to a boil, stirring. Cook, stirring, until thickened and smooth. Stir in the mustard and cheddar cheese, then season with salt and pepper.

5 In a large, rectangular ovenproof dish, make a layer of meat sauce, then lasagna noodles, then Parmesan cheese, and repeat the layers. Pour the cheese sauce over the layers, covering them completely, and sprinkle with Parmesan cheese. Bake in the preheated oven for 30 minutes, or until the top is golden brown and bubbling. Serve immediately.

GRANDMA'S TIP
This dish is complicated. To cheat a little, you can buy a prepared cheese sauce to cut down on the preparation time.

Spaghetti & Meatballs

SERVES 4

INGREDIENTS

- 2 tablespoons olive oil, plus extra for brushing
- 1 onion, finely diced
- 4 garlic cloves, minced
- ½ teaspoon dried Italian herbs, such as basil, parsley, oregano, and/or marjoram
- ½ day-old ciabatta loaf, crusts removed
- ¼ cup whole milk
- 2 pounds ground beef, well chilled
- 2 extra-large eggs, lightly beaten
- ⅓ cup chopped fresh flat-leaf parsley
- ⅔ cup Parmesan cheese, grated, plus extra to serve
- 2 teaspoons salt
- 1 teaspoon pepper
- 6 ½ cups marinara or other prepared pasta sauce
- 1 cup water
- 1 pound thick dried spaghetti
- salt and pepper

1 Heat the olive oil in a saucepan. Add the onion, garlic, and a pinch of salt, cover, and cook over medium–low heat for 6–7 minutes, until softened and golden. Remove the pan from the heat, stir in the dried herbs, and let cool to room temperature.

2 Tear the bread into small chunks and put into a food processor, in batches, depending on the size of the machine. Pulse to make fine bread crumbs—you'll need 3 cups in total. Put the crumbs into a bowl, toss with the milk, and let soak for 10 minutes.

3 Preheat the oven to 425°F. Brush a baking sheet with oil.

4 Put the beef, eggs, parsley, cheese, bread crumbs, cooled onion mixture, 2 teaspoons of salt, and 1 teaspoon of pepper into a bowl. Mix well with your hands until thoroughly combined.

5 Dampen your hands and roll pieces of the mixture into balls about the size of a golf ball. Put them on the prepared sheet and bake in the preheated oven for 20 minutes. Meanwhile, pour the pasta sauce into a saucepan, stir in the water, and bring to simmering point. When the meatballs are done, transfer them into the hot sauce, reduce the heat to low, cover, and simmer gently for 45 minutes.

6 Bring a large saucepan of lightly salted water to a boil, add the spaghetti, curling it around the pan as it softens. Bring back to a boil and cook according to the package directions, until tender but still firm to the bite.

7 Drain the spaghetti in a colander and transfer to a large serving dish. Ladle some of the sauce from the meatballs over it and toss to coat. Top with the meatballs and the remaining sauce, sprinkle with cheese, and serve immediately.

GRANDMA'S TIP
For the best flavor, store tomatoes in a basket in a cool place where air can circulate, instead of in the refrigerator.

Asparagus & Tomato Tart

SERVES 4

INGREDIENTS

- butter, for greasing
- 1 sheet store-bought rolled dough pie crust, thawed, if frozen
- 1 bunch thin asparagus spears
- 9 cups fresh spinach leaves
- 3 extra-large eggs, beaten
- ⅔ cup heavy cream
- 1 garlic clove, crushed
- 10 small cherry tomatoes, halved
- handful fresh basil, chopped
- ¼ cup freshly grated Parmesan cheese
- salt and pepper

1 Preheat the oven to 375°F. Grease a 9-inch tart pan with butter, then roll out the dough and use to line the pan.

2 Trim off any excess dough at the rim, prick the bottom with a fork, cover with a piece of parchment paper, and fill with pie weights or dried beans. Bake the shell in the preheated oven for 20–30 minutes, until lightly browned. Remove from the oven and let cool slightly. Reduce the oven temperature to 350°F.

3 Meanwhile, bend the asparagus spears until they snap, and discard the woody ends. Bring a large saucepan of lightly salted water to a boil, add the asparagus, and blanch for 1 minute, then remove and drain. Add the spinach to a saucepan of boiling water, then remove immediately and drain well.

4 Mix together the eggs, cream, and garlic and season with salt and pepper. Lay the blanched spinach at the bottom of the pastry shell, add the asparagus and the tomatoes, cut side up, in any arrangement you prefer, sprinkle with the basil, then pour the egg mixture on top.

5 Transfer to the oven and bake for about 35 minutes, or until the filling has set. Sprinkle the cheese on top and let cool to room temperature before serving.

GRANDMA'S TIP
This is a great dish to make for summer picnics and backyard parties. The ingredients are interchangeable with other crisp spring and summer vegetables.

Steak & French Fries

SERVES 4

INGREDIENTS

- 4 tenderloin steaks, about 8 ounces each
- 4 teaspoons Tabasco sauce
- salt and pepper

FRENCH FRIES

- 4 large russet potatoes, peeled and cut into sticks
- 2 tablespoons sunflower oil

HERB BUTTER

- 1 stick unsalted butter, softened
- ¼ cup of fresh herbs of your choice, such as basil, flat-leaf parsley, chervil, or watercress
- 1 garlic clove, minced

1 To make the French fries, preheat the oven to 400°F. Rinse the sticks under cold running water and then dry well on a clean dish towel. Place in a bowl, add the oil, and toss together until coated.

2 Spread the French fries on a baking sheet and cook in the preheated oven for 40–45 minutes, turning once, until golden.

3 To make the herb butter, put all the ingredients in a small bowl and beat with a fork until fully incorporated.

Cover with plastic wrap and let chill in the refrigerator until required.

4 Preheat a ridged grill pan to high. Sprinkle each steak with 1 teaspoon of the Tabasco sauce, rubbing it in well. Season with salt and pepper.

5 Cook the steaks in the preheated pan for 2½ minutes each side for rare, 4 minutes each side for medium, and 6 minutes each side for well done. Transfer to warm serving plates and serve immediately, topped with some herb butter and accompanied by the French fries.

GRANDMA'S TIP

To test for doneness, press the steak gently with the tip of your finger. Rare should be soft and supple, well done firm, and medium in between.

Roasted Chicken

SERVES 6

INGREDIENTS

- 5-pound chicken
- 4 tablespoons salted butter
- 2 tablespoons chopped fresh lemon thyme
- 1 lemon, quartered
- ½ cup white wine
- salt and pepper

1 Preheat the oven to 425°F.

2 Make sure the chicken is clean, wiping it inside and out with paper, towels then place in a roasting pan.

3 In a bowl, soften the butter with a fork, mix in the thyme, and season well with salt and pepper.

4 Rub the chicken all over with the herb butter, inside and out, and place the lemon pieces inside the body cavity. Pour the wine over the chicken.

5 Roast in the center of the preheated oven for 20 minutes. Reduce the temperature to 375°F and continue to roast for an additional 1¼ hours, basting frequently. Cover with aluminum foil if the skin begins to brown too much. If the liquid in the pan dries out, add a little more wine or water.

6 Test that the chicken is cooked by piercing the thickest part of the leg with a sharp knife and making sure the juices run clear. Remove from the oven.

7 Place the chicken on a warm serving plate, cover with aluminum foil, and let rest for 10 minutes before carving.

8 Place the roasting pan on the stove and bubble the pan juices gently over low heat, until they have reduced and are thick and glossy. Season with salt and pepper.

9 Serve the chicken with the pan juices.

GRANDMA'S TIP
To give more depth and a touch of sweetness to the finished dish, add a generous splash of Marsala to the pan juices when reducing them.

Roasted Potatoes

SERVES 6
INGREDIENTS

- 6 large russet or white round potatoes or 3 pounds new potatoes, peeled and cut into even chunks
- 3 tablespoons dripping, goose fat, duck fat, or olive oil
- salt

1 Preheat the oven to 425°F.

2 Bring a large saucepan of lightly salted water to a boil, add the potatoes, bring back to a boil, and cook for 5–7 minutes. The potatoes should still be firm. Remove from the heat.

3 Meanwhile, add the dripping to a roasting pan and place the pan in the preheated oven.

4 Drain the potatoes well and return them to the saucepan. Cover with the lid and firmly shake the pan so that the surface of the potatoes is roughened to help give a much crisper texture.

5 Remove the roasting pan from the oven and carefully transfer the potatoes to the hot oil. Baste them to make sure they are all coated with the oil.

6 Roast at the top of the oven for 45–50 minutes, until they are browned all over and thoroughly crisp. Turn the potatoes and baste only once during the process or the crunchy edges will be destroyed.

7 Carefully transfer the potatoes from the roasting pan to a warm serving dish. Sprinkle with a little salt and serve immediately.

GRANDMA'S GUILTY PLEASURE

Whole Roasted Rib of Beef

SERVES 8
INGREDIENTS

- olive oil, for rubbing
- 6½-pound standing rib roast
- ½ tablespoon all-purpose flour
- I cup beef stock
- I cup red wine

YORKSHIRE PUDDING

- 2 cups all-purpose flour, sifted
- 6 eggs
- ½ teaspoon salt
- 2½ cups whole milk
- 2 tablespoons vegetable oil or lard

ROASTED POTATOES

- 4½ pounds russet, white round, or new potatoes, peeled
- ⅓ cup sunflower oil, goose fat, or duck fat
- salt and pepper

TO SERVE

- glazed carrots
- steamed broccoli
- horseradish sauce
- mustard

1 For the Yorkshire pudding, mix together the flour, eggs, and salt in a bowl, then gradually add the milk as you stir it with a whisk. When smooth, set aside but don't chill.

2 For the roasted potatoes, bring a large saucepan of lightly salted water to a boil, add the potatoes, bring back to a boil, and cook for 10 minutes. Drain the potatoes and toss them in oil and salt and pepper. Put them in a roasting pan in a single layer.

3 Preheat the oven to 425°F. Put a 16 × 10-inch roasting pan in the bottom of the oven to warm for the Yorkshire pudding.

4 Rub a generous amount of olive oil and salt and pepper into the beef, then place in a roasting pan. Transfer to the preheated oven and roast for 30 minutes.

5 Reduce the temperature to 325°F. Transfer the potatoes to the oven and roast with the beef for 60 minutes. Remove the beef from the oven and increase the oven temperature to 425°F. Cover the beef with aluminum foil and let rest for at least 30 minutes.

6 Remove the roasting pan from the bottom of the oven and add the vegetable oil. Put it back in the oven for 5 minutes, then remove it and add the Yorkshire pudding batter. Put it back in the hot oven for about 20 minutes.

7 Meanwhile, make the gravy. Remove the beef from the pan and stir the flour into the leftover juices, add the stock and wine, then simmer over medium heat unt reduced by about half.

8 Remove the Yorkshire pudding and the potatoes from the oven. Cut the Yorkshire Pudding into 8 pieces. Cut the rib bones off the meat and carve the beef. Serve with the gravy, potatoes Yorkshire pudding, carrots, broccoli, horseradish sauce, and mustard.

HEART WARMING FOOD

Sweet & Sour Red Cabbage

SERVES 6–8
INGREDIENTS

- 1 head of red cabbage (about 1¾ pounds)
- 2 tablespoons olive oil
- 2 onions, finely sliced
- 1 garlic clove, chopped
- 2 small Granny Smith apples, peeled, cored, and sliced
- 2 tablespoons packed brown sugar
- ½ teaspoon ground cinnamon
- 1 teaspoon crushed juniper berries
- whole nutmeg, for grating
- 2 tablespoons red wine vinegar
- grated rind and juice of 1 orange
- 2 tablespoons red currant or cranberry jelly
- salt and pepper

1 Cut the cabbage into quarters, remove the core in the middle, and finely shred the leaves.

2 Heat the oil in a large saucepan over medium heat and add the cabbage, onions, garlic, and apples. Stir in the sugar, cinnamon, and juniper berries and grate a quarter of the nutmeg into the pan.

3 Pour in the vinegar and orange juice and add the orange rind.

4 Stir well and season with salt and pepper. The pan will be full but the volume of the cabbage will reduce during cooking.

5 Cook over medium heat, stirring occasionally, until the cabbage is just tender but still has bite. This will take 10–15 minutes, depending on how finely the cabbage is sliced.

6 Stir in the red currant jelly, then taste and adjust the seasoning, adding salt and pepper, if necessary. Serve immediately.

GRANDMA'S TIP
This is the perfect winter dish and is the classic accompaniment to roasted pork. It also goes well with ham at Christmas, or sausages, any day of the week.

Poached Salmon

IMPRESS THE FAMILY

SERVES 6
INGREDIENTS

- 6–8-pound whole salmon (head on)
- 3 tablespoons salt
- 3 bay leaves
- 10 black peppercorns
- 1 onion, peeled and sliced
- 1 lemon, sliced
- lemon wedges, to serve

1 Wipe the salmon thoroughly inside and out with paper towels, then use the back of a chef's knife to remove any scales that might still be on the skin. Remove the fins with a pair of scissors and trim the tail. Some people prefer to cut off the head but, traditionally, salmon is served with the head on.

2 Place the salmon on the two-handled rack that comes with a fish poacher, then place it in the poacher. Fill the poacher with enough cold water to cover the salmon adequately. Sprinkle with the salt, bay leaves, and peppercorns, along with the onion and lemon slices.

3 Place the poacher over low heat, over two burners, and slowly bring just to a boil.

4 Cover and simmer gently. To serve cold, simmer for only 2 minutes, remove from the heat, and let cool in the liquid for about 2 hours with the lid on. To serve hot, simmer for 6–8 minutes and let stand in the hot water for 15 minutes before removing. Remove the bay leaves and serve with lemon wedges for squeezing over the fish.

Mashed Potatoes

SERVES 4

INGREDIENTS

- 8 Yukon gold or russet potatoes (about 2 pounds), peeled and cut into even chunks
- 4 tablespoons salted butter
- 3 tablespoons hot milk
- salt and pepper

1 Bring a large saucepan of lightly salted water to a boil, add the potatoes, bring back to a boil, and cook for 20–25 minutes, until they are tender. Test with the point of a knife, making sure you test right to the middle if you don't like lumpy mashed potatoes.

2 Remove the pan from the heat and drain the potatoes. Return the potatoes to the hot pan and mash with a vegetable masher until smooth.

3 Add the butter and continue to mash until it is all mixed in, then add the milk (it is better hot because the potatoes absorb it more quickly to produce a creamier mash).

4 Taste the mashed potatoes and season with salt and pepper, if necessary. Serve immediately.

FEEL-BETTER FOOD

Roasted Butternut Squash

SERVES 4

INGREDIENTS

- 1 butternut squash
- 1 onion, chopped
- 2–3 garlic cloves, crushed
- 4 small tomatoes, chopped
- 1¼ cups chopped cremini mushrooms
- ⅓ cup drained, rinsed, and coarsely chopped canned lima beans
- 1 cup grated zucchini
- 1 tablespoon chopped fresh oregano, plus extra to garnish
- 2 tablespoons tomato paste
- 1¼ cups water
- 4 scallions, trimmed and chopped
- 1 tablespoon Worcestershire sauce, or to taste
- pepper

1 Preheat the oven to 375°F. Prick the squash all over with the tip of a sharp knife, then bake for 40 minutes, or until tender. Remove from the oven and let rest until cool enough to handle.

2 Cut the squash in half, scoop out and discard the seeds, then scoop out some of the flesh, making hollows in both halves. Chop the scooped-out flesh and put in a bowl. Place the two squash halves side by side in a large roasting pan.

3 Add the onion, garlic, tomatoes, and mushrooms to the squash flesh in the bowl. Add the lima beans, zucchini, and oregano, season with pepper, and mix well. Spoon the filling into the two halves of the squash, packing it down as firmly as possible.

4 Mix the tomato paste with the water, scallions, and Worcestershire sauce in a small bowl and pour around the squash.

5 Cover loosely with a large sheet of aluminum foil and bake for 30 minutes, or until piping hot. Serve in warm bowls, garnished with some chopped oregano.

GRANDMA'S TIP
Butternut squash is a versatile winter fruit. It can be roasted or cooked and pureed to make a soup, or used in casseroles, breads, and even muffins.